HOMAGE TO
DAFYDD AP GWILYM

Dafydd ap Gwilym's Yew Tree, Strata Florida Churchyard,
reproduced by permission of The National Library of Wales, Aberystwyth

HOMAGE TO DAFYDD AP GWILYM

Martin Green

Welsh Studies
Volume 9

The Edwin Mellen Press
Lewiston/Queenston/Lampeter

Library of Congress Cataloging-in-Publication Data

This volume has been registered with The Library of Congress.

This is volume 9 in the continuing series
Welsh Studies
Volume 9 ISBN 0-7734-9318-2
We S Series ISBN 0-88946-479-0

A CIP catalog record for this book
is available from the British Library.

Copyright © 1993 The Edwin Mellen Press

All rights reserved. For information contact

The Edwin Mellen Press
Box 450
Lewiston, New York
USA 14092

The Edwin Mellen Press
Box 67
Queenston, Ontario
CANADA L0S 1L0

Edwin Mellen Press, Ltd.
Lampeter, Dyfed, Wales
UNITED KINGDOM SA48 7DY

Printed in the United States of America

LIBRARY
ALMA COLLEGE
ALMA, MICHIGAN

CONTENTS

Author's Notes vii
Introduction ix

Poems:
Seagull 1
The Pilgrimage 3
Storm 6
Snow 7
Wind 9
The Lark 11
Winter 14
Funeral Rites 15
The Assignation 16
Dawn 18
Secret 20
Llanbadarn 22
The Lock 24
The Grey Friar 26
Green Mass 30
Doppelgänger 31
The Bog 33
The Loan 34
The Mirror 36
The Hard Road 37
The Mouse 39
The Window 40
Manafon Dingle 42

AUTHOR'S NOTE

In the opinion of many, including George Borrow, Dafydd ap Gwilym is the greatest poet of Wales. I came across his work when I was living in Wales, through a prose translation by Nigel Heseltine. Sometime after I left Wales, I was visited by Dafydd's spirit and I did the following versions in the space of two weeks.

INTRODUCTION

As we learn from the Author's Note, there are many, including George Borrow, who regard Dafydd ap Gwilym as the greatest poet in Wales. Others would favour William Williams of Pantycelyn, that indefatigable writer of hymns in the eighteenth century. Both were the products of an awakening in the life and culture of their people. Over the decades both have been in competition among the Welsh for recognition as the 'best'. One need not be surprised that there are others also, as the Welsh have invariably taken pleasure and delight in competitions from a very early time, more especially literary competitions. They produced the Eisteddfod, a term now familiar the world over. Initially, this institution was meant for a small circle of bards who met to compete and discuss matters relating to poetry. Later, in the last century and in this, it developed as a public institution for the benefit and pleasure of all and sundry. And we still have it and cherish it.

Dafydd ap Gwilym belonged to the late Middle Ages. He hailed from Dyfed and Ceredigion, and lived in the years c.1320–c.1380. The middle years of the century were probably his most productive period, although it has to be recognized that we sadly lack details regarding the events of his life, as most of the information available is derived from his poetry. As for the latter, it has to be admitted that there was over the years considerable confusion and controversy, and it was only recently that a serious, scholarly attempt was made to establish the canon of his work. This was done in a sustained study extending over many years by the distinguished author and scholar Sir Thomas

Parry who published his *Gwaith Dafydd ap Gwilym* (The Work of Dafydd ap Gwilym) in 1952. Over thirty years later we have the contributions of another distinguished scholar, Dr Rachel Bromwich. She has contributed brilliantly to our understanding and appreciation of this great artist whose command of language and pleasing and easy acquaintance with the world of the imagination has attracted the attention, admiration and dedication of scholars and devotees of the muse beyond the areas of Wales and the Celtic world generally. Dafydd describes himself as a member of the *clêr*. How much credence we can give to this is doubtful, but we learn in other countries of the *clerici vagrantes* or 'wandering scholars', and Dafydd at one time may have qualified for minor religious orders. He must have been introduced to the 'two cultures', the native bardic tradition taking us back eventually to the sixth century, and the language and poetry and romances of the Anglo-Norman clearly reflecting influences from outside, the two being very frequently blended. Over all Wales he found a welcome and joy in the taverns of the Norman boroughs and in the *plastai* of his cultivated Welsh friends.

The primary appeal of Welsh poetry from very early times has always been to the ear rather than to the eye; it is worth noting that medieval poetry was accompanied on the harp. With the blossoming of Dafydd's verse in the fourteenth century, there came into prominence a new metre known as *cywydd deuair hirion*, usually abbreviated *cywydd*. The *cywydd* consists of a couplet of seven syllabled lines rhyming unrhythmically, i.e. an accented final syllable rhymes with an unaccented final syllable, either of which may precede the other in the first line of the couplet. Dafydd's *cywydd* is normally between thirty and sixty lines in length. In every line there is full *cynghanedd* or 'harmony'. *Cynghanedd* which developed during the twelfth and thirteenth centuries denotes the regularized pattern of alliteration combined with internal rhyme. Any one of four types may be employed in a line.

Although Dafydd was familiar with old time-honoured themes and techniques, and composed some religious verse, he is to be credited mainly with the introduction of new themes, which in the main relate to love and nature. There were two women in his life, or so we are led to believe! One was Morfudd, married to *Y Bwa Bach*, 'The Little Hunchback', also known as

Yr Eiddig, 'The Jealous One', already a conventional figure in European poetry. The other was Dyddgu, who was aristocratic and virginal. Both seem to have existed, but not necessarily in the form and in the role in which they are portrayed by Dafydd. Finally, Dafydd had a friend and patron, Ifor Hael, Ifor the Generous, for whom he composed seven praise-poems.

Dafydd was an earlier contemporary of Chaucer and was probably born in Brogynin in the parish of Llanbadarn Fawr, a few miles north-east of Aberystwyth. His father was Gwilym Gam ap Gwilym, and his descent could be traced ultimately to a certain Gwynfardd Dyfed. There is evidence linking him firmly with Dyfed, and one notes the reference of his fellow-poet Madog Benfras to him as *eos* Dyfed, 'the nightingale of Dyfed'. His uncle Hywelyn ap Gwilym, the constable of Newcastle Emlyn, appears to have had a powerful educational influence on him in early life. The prevailing view has been that Dafydd was buried in the Cistercian abbey of Strata Florida, but there does seem to be some slight evidence for connecting his burial with the Premonstratensian abbey of Talyllychau to the north of Llandeilo.

D. Simon Evans

SEAGULL

White seagull on rising tide
As snow white or as white of moon
Beauty as sun in his full pride
Or crystal salt upon a dune.

Fly lightly over bounteous sea
Wing-fishing over fertile waves
Sea-flower come and fly for me
Beyond the deep and water graves.

You are my white flying-letter
A nun riding the convent sea
Go find she than whom none better
At castle-camp your fame will be.

Look, my seagull-letter, find
The brightest shining maid of all
In that far castle-camp confined
From you on her let my words fall.

Tell her this, I am for her choice
Go to her now, the very one
And take her with a winning voice
My beauteous messenger-gone!

O my courteous courier of white
Your wings must take these words I sign
I am her love by day and night
And I shall die unless she's mine.

O brother men, whoever loved
With such a love? Merlin more hot,
Taliesin by some creature moved
More beauteous than she? No, not!

Jewels of fine-grain-on-copper-fall
Is my beauty's wondrous beauty
In Christendom behind no wall
One whose face is as God's bounty.

My wingéd messenger, my bird
You must know that I'll surely die
Unless you bring me some kind word
From whom I love, who floods my eye.

THE PILGRIMAGE

Radiance, promise, dawn
Delight everywhere born
Morfudd the nun my love
From Mona flies this dove
A pilgrimage oblique
To Mynyw for to seek
Forgiveness from St Non
And to St David gone
For arrow words that killed
Her lover, poet-skilled
A slender penitent
Wanting passion-content
For forgiveness she has flowers
Culled from her lover's hours
From guilt of this young man
Who sings no more, nor can
So with grief and loving gone
Her journey pale and wan
The heart of Morfudd sealed is
Her lips a silent quiz
Journey be safe for her
Let no hindrance deter.

Leave lovely Mona's isle?
It is as if colour's smile
Is drained from healthy cheeks
Left white as snow-clad peaks
Lord Jesus let her crossing
Be saved the hard storm-tossing
Kind Straits of Menai pass
This love and golden lass
Traeth-Mawr your tide let ebb

Receive a jewel honey-fed
Traeth-Mawr, Traeth-Bach estuaries
Like joined lovers' hands and knees
Let my delight journey safe
The comely gilded sea-waif
I make a prayer for your calm
Great Arthro please your balm;
The price of a whole farm for your fee
To wave-carry the estuary
That one of sweetest mouth
Over tides-dangerous Barmouth!

Dee Dovey's wine-dark flood
Shivering water take this bud
Nine waves carry this sweet
To sweet St David's seat
For your best honour Rheidol
Make passage for this human doll
And Ystwyth grant a crossing fair
Between your bank's most pleasing pair
Rowdy Aeron bubbling nimble
Gleaming as a moving thimble
Bright silver let my golden love
Pass through gentle like hand glove
Teifi golden springing water
Let pass this mother's daughter
Pass your pleasing grace
Towards another sainted place
Carry to river mouth strong
Her journey do no wrong.

Of all happiness Holy Mother
Robed in purple like the heather
Living between Mynyw and the sea
Though my love has murdered me
Let her go a lengthy while
Before she's called to justice' stile
May Mary's hand of charity
Grant all lovers' parity
Forgive my gentlest seabird
For murder with a cruel word
Though I should defend my own
I forgive all ills she's sown.

STORM

A loving word, a stately couch embowered
Serenaded by cuckoo and by thrush
A Brecon lass, myself, we were empowered
By love and May to hold ourselves love's crush.
She of the brown eye lay with me and I
Was come to peace, when bang! the thunder struck
And up she leapt my little darling, shy,
She dashed away with many a frightened cluck.
From far beyond Builth the roaring of a bull
Sounded the thunder as the lightning jagged.
Fire and loud roaring fought my heart, to pull
It from my side, and I in terror sagged,
Beset by witches, wrapped in soaken wool
My amours stifled like a husband nagged!

SNOW

No sleep at night
When world is white
Even a girl will not
Draw me from my cot
While white plague rages
Blank making field's pages
She who entices me
Tell her to go and flee
I don't want miller's white
To button my coat tight
After New Year wear fur
Hermit foil love's spur.

God has white-washed world
Earth and branches pearled
With snow crystal cold
Covered grass, moss, mould
Heaven's flour shaken over all
Like April's blossom-fall
A cold veil hidden all ground
Sheep disguised in pound
As lumps of white whiteness
Under cold weight press.

Everywhere trees bear down
Under white snow crown
A coat of frozen pain
Whitely covers plain
The soil of fields ploughed
Frozen-flour showered.

Frozen foam fleeces fall
From flock clouds small
Across the north of Wales
The white rage sails
Like swarms of white bees
Buzzing round the trees
God throws down feather
And we hide below
Under chaffs of snow.

White powder drifts now
Where we sang the plough
Tell me someone why
In cold January
They throw white dust
Sawn from white-plank lust
From flour-mill shaving wood
Covering white nature's good?

They wear white silver cloaks
Who play these powder jokes
The snow coat that traps
Has the whole earth in wraps
Hidden valley, ditches, fields
To nothing its whiteness yields
A great graveyard
Even living frozen hard
My country white
By day and night
From sea to sea
When will soft rain
Make world green again?

WIND

What a wonderful phenomenon
Going where you will in the wild sky
Without feet or wings, riding on
Nothing! From whence do you fly
      What northern valley hie?

Fly for me across bright Aeron
Don't listen to that hunchback's foul words
Who puts a lie my very soul upon
And makes me flee like wounded bird
      Driven alone and to exile gone!

You are free, above all you play,
No force can hold you, no armed man
No powerful government make you pay
For scorning all below, wonderful phenomenon
      Subject to no-one, none to obey!

No horse, bridge over stream, boat
Need you call to your aid
You who fear no man, no sheriff's coat
Nor none dare fright you with lackey's paid
      — Invisible too, like winter's stoat!

But what might you have, by God's will
When you loose boulders, break down trees!
Your loud trumpeting all men fill
With wonder, who sit with quaking knees —
      And your huge travels cross the seas!

With your tumultuous voice
Breaking ships' masts against white waves,
Who flies through time, wherever choice
Takes you, to whom all else are slaves,
      Find her tonight, across dead men's graves!

She whom I gave my love
Who holds me a prisoner fast
Go to her father's house, with mailed glove
Smote down the door with your strength, cast
      Aside who might protect my dove!

Tell gentle Morfudd with your loud roar,
Lowered softly to a pleased tone,
'As long as breath's in me I'll adore,
My face without your love is bone' –
      If she's still true – and alone!

You will know her from on high
Morfudd of the shining yellow hair
Drop to her quietly like a sigh
Descend as do wings on air,
      Who is your sweeter part, your care!

THE LARK

The lark sings high praises
    the morning to fill
From his high house
    his song brings April.

What a sweet voice is
    above hazel trees
And you a little brown bird
    so modest, who flies
        with such ease

Ah, what but a pleasant office
    preaching word's leaves
In the heart of God's house
    you're safe in His eaves!

High above all you sail
    passionately singing songs
Oh sweet almost-smallest bird
    what a gift of tongues!

Be brother mine, go to she who walks
    with the brightness of moon
Go to Gwynedd and bring me
    her sweet kisses back soon!

I am spellbound for her,
    her stars surround me
Go above these stars
    for favours, flyer free!

Daylight song tutor
        your sanctuary's God's charity
Which falls as does rain
        with just partiality.

As all creatures praise love
        so you praise God
Let all below be showered
        beneath heaven's sod!

From your tiny grey-brown body
        issues such voice
To all who seek God's chapel
        by choice

By your skilful song
        bring me sweet kisses won
Simply by your mellifluous
        syllables won!

High on the clear longest days
        you are supported
By God's seeming grace
        and we below transported

Lord of all the huge
        intangible wondrous sky
Go now to where my love is,
        go fly!

Tell her how I would lie with her
        with her always
And be a thorn in Jealousy's side
        night, noon, days!

Though Jealousy may wish
        to kill you for your news
Such is your worth he knows
        that for God you choose!

With your courage then
        we have no need to fear
Your cage is without bars
        your flight without peer!

You may fly out of all
        cruel harm's way above
The stumbling world below,
        of me and my love!

He who would bring you
        down with his bow
Fly mockingly above
        dodge his sharpest arrow!

WINTER

Unhappy the man who in winter loves
His desire's great, his prayers without reward
Lovers in winter are hands without gloves
Hopping from foot to foot, even bones bored;
The only warmth, summer's memories.
As I spilled from the tavern most wretched
In case, amidst the passion-daunting freeze
I find my love with another man fetched,
I found myself under icicled eaves,
The cold like arrows piercing my body;
Inside they woke from my incautious sneeze
And Jealousy leapt from his lover's ease
Thinking his purse threatened; the foul toady
Shouted alarms, me cringing on my knees.

FUNERAL RITES

It is by your beauty I am destroyed
Forehead lily, a slender wand of gold
O Blessed Mary! from lack of you I'm void
Feared to take sight of you, your people told
Of my desire would vengeance seek on me.
Your beauty fatal, my death at your door.
My funeral bower shall be the wooded trees
My shroud the leaves, my bier the forest floor.
Nightingales shall sing me to my bower
The trees intone the solemn Latin tongue
Pallbearers be at this my final hour.
Gwynedd's pleasant country my grave and song
Beyond all harm from Jealousy's power
Llan Eos my paradise, my last bed long!

THE ASSIGNATION

It came to pass we reached the chosen town
My servant and myself, we settled down,
A decent inn where lodging could be had
I summonsed dinner for myself, the lad,
But what should I espy, slender and fine,
A pretty young girl, ah she must be mine!
I'll set her up a treat with food and drink
How pleasant love becomes when it's well fed
And afterwards, what better than to bed?
I was in luck, my invitation charmed,
Had my companion totally disarmed.
We made an assignation then and there
That I would seek her out no matter where
When all the travellers were fast asleep;
To her on stockinged feet I would make creep.
She had dark eyebrows and a raven's thatch
The darkest eyes to make a perfect match!

When all about me snored upon their backs
I set off carefully, for boards with cracks,
Then I stumbled on a damned obstruction
Some awful Englishmen with foul diction,
Three lodged together in a stinking pit,
Pedlars with packs and none with any wit,
Hicken, Shockin and Shack or some such names
Who thought I was after stealing their games.
'Some bloody Welshman creeping in the dark,'
A right one shouted, some nightwatchman's nark!
The scummy-mouthed unpleasant English louts
All fighting in the dark and raising shouts.
Not exactly nimble, bereft of light
I caught my shin a blow in my blind flight.

Of all my escapades this was not best
The inn turned upside down where had been rest.
I cursed the ostler who had left that stool
Against my shin, the rogue, the knave, the fool!
Like maybug in a room I crashed about
Followed here and there by many a shout
Away I went into the night's embrace
Pursued, abused, the first one in the race —
And me a poet honoured by my words!
For sweet Jesus' charity I prayed
Surrounded by ferocious dogs that bayed;
By goodness' of all saints I got away
Misfortune picked on me for sure today!

DAWN

Sighing deeply for last night
I am; it was too short for us
A week's love we shared with delight
    A week and overplus!

Last night I encompassed all,
Heaven's candles lit the snow
And every time I went to fall
    She met me with a glow.

Triumph upon ecstasy
I held her in my arms, when Oh!
— Her hair falling abundantly —
    'It's dawn and you must go!

My darling and my honey dear
You must arise and slip away
While I lie trembling in fear
    It is the break of day!'

'Not so,' I said, 'I see the moon
Keeping her vigil in the sky.'
'But I can hear the blackbird's tune
    And morning must be nigh.'

'That's not a bird but just the stream
Singing down upon the stones.'
'I hear the dogs, that's not a dream
    Be quick and rouse your bones!'

'No more excuses my poet
Fool's wisdom brings the bigger grief
Get up and go or you'll know it
    Dogs bite poet and thief.'

'Fear not, my flight is swift as deer
No dog can catch me when I go
I'll leave you now without a fear
    Only my heels will show.'

'Goodbye, sweet poet, will you come,
God willing, when all's clear again;
Surely, unfinished, you have some
    Lovers' words yet to pen?'

'My lady of the night you know
I am your sweetest nightingale
And when night falls again I'll show
    The bird who sings love's tale.'

SECRET

About my secret love I'm bold
Bravely the secret I flaunted it
Not like a boor, everyone told;
Now I'll write it like a poet.

Who loves in secret loves the best
We walked together she and I
And no-one knew where we took rest
We joked and we were very sly.

We played at outlaws for a joke
The joke became too true and now
We have to move without love's yoke
For slander weighs our precious bough.

Pleased we were our love was hid
We revelled in its secrecy
And now we have to close the lid
Lest it leaks out to Jealousy.

A joy to dally by the sea
Or stray within the leafy wood
Or pass the day silently
Loving or not as the mood would.

No better way a girl can pass
The time, than in the woody groves
Or lie upon the mossy grass
Playing he loves-me-not, he loves!

All that was the best of times
Nothing more precious ever could be
For perfect I cannot find rhymes
Words fail poet, silence be!

LLANBADARN

Like a fork I am
Doubled like a hoop
Laughter at my very name
A cockerel in a coop
Crowing without triumph
No hens to my will
Have I got a hump
That all the women spill
Laughing from the church
As at some popinjay?
And I in love so much
With Carwy and Criewy
Boundless my passion
Enough for two girls
And what harm is love
Deep in the wood?
No Sunday passed
In Llanbadarn
But I transgressed
Both God and man
Turning my fine hat
Away from the altar
To gaze at the girls
Over my shoulder.
One beauty whispered
So I could hear
'Look at that whey-faced
Self-opinionated fool
With his feathers falling.
Why does he stare so
— As if he might pass
Muster on a wet night?'

'Well,' said her friend,
'He can stare as long
As he likes at us
From noon till tomorrow
He'll get no joy
From you or I.'
What a nasty blast
From such a pretty girl,
And me so well knit!
Must I be a hermit
Walking ever alone
Live in a cave
No girl of my own?

THE LOCK

Sick I am of loving you
A lock is on the house
And surely this is new?

Let me through your door
For God's sweet sake
I couldn't love you more!

It is you I have sung
And widely celebrated
Would you have me hung?

My clumsy fingers broke
The damned ungainly latch
And hope went up in smoke!

I heard the lock go click
Do you hear me now?
What a deceitful trick!

Morfudd my chaste jewel
The nurse of all deceit
You have me for your fool.

Against the wall I sleep
A stone my pillow
You must hold my love cheap.

Bad the weather that falls
In torrents from the roof
Uncomfortable your walls.

The rain is not more cruel
Than your ingratitude
In your heart no fuel!

I would be better dead
Than half-frozen alive
Stones only for my bed.

Even my creator
Could not use me worse
Than my heart's torturer.

Even in Caernarvon Jail
It was not half as bad
A roof, a crust, some ale.

Here I am outside
Your charity withheld
And frozen by your pride.

Life cannot sustain me
Outside your frozen lock
But madness to seize me!

THE GREY FRIAR

It is a pity for me
        That she whose praises I sing
Who holds court in the trees
        Knows not the day's converse
Which was most flattering
I had with the grey friar
        Talking of love and verse.
        You were my sole desire
I told him, and you were
        A most cruel mistress
And had given me no hope
        But spurned my finest trope.

As well as telling him
        What a lovely girl
You were, both dark and slim
        I told him of your brown curls
And how you'd been so cruel
And I singing your beauty
        Through the whole of Wales
        As if it were my duty;
Between me and the wall
        I'd lie with you I said
Like Eve at Adam's fall.

The good brother said thus:
        I will give you good advice
Only between God and us
        Your love is sweet and nice
But it is too long you've craved
This paragon of yours.

Time will knock the doors
    That open for your soul
As your flesh looks at the jaws
    Of Death. Think on the whole
Of other things, the sins
    Which are not childish whims!

So rhyme no more poet
    Rather at your prayers
The good God will reck it
    While you are praising hairs
Your rhymes and elegies
Are nothing but bawling
    And idle flatteries
Flesh should be scorning
    Sinful to praise the flesh
It's He on high for praise
    Whom all souls doth refresh.

I answered then the good friar
    For every word he said:
God is not cruel as old men are
    And love says grace in bed
He will not cut off gentle souls
Whose love is womankind
    The wedding bed extols
More than the funeral knell
Three things the world doth love
    Woman, good weather, health
These things are not above
    Nor are they loved by stealth!

The fairest flower of heaven
    Apart from Christ the King
Is a fair maid at even
    Nor does it wrong to sing
Man is born of woman
From her it is he fell
    Gladness falls from heaven
Misery comes from Hell
    It would be profanity
If mankind did not love
His worldly nativity
    As much as Queen above!

And songs bring joy to all
    The old the young the sick
And songs are prayerful
    The poets have the trick
To sing for supper's mead
So does the good priest beg
    For his satchel of bread
And rhymes are next to hymns
Are not the psalms of David
    But poems for great God?
Nor does God provide just
    Only a humble crust.

There's time to eat and pray
    And songs are for the feast
To pleasure ladies gay
    There's worship in the yeast
Paters are said in church
For paradise hereafter
    Yscuthach spoke the truth
    'A full house, a happy face,
A sad face, bitterness and ill'
    Everything has its place
And God must have His will
    The priest, poet and ploughman till.

As some love holiness
    And prayerful isolation
Others come to gladness
    And sing their delectation
And so my holy brother
Singing is no great sin
    And when men crave the pater
    As much as the poet's song
I'll gladly give up poems
    Say pater all day long
Till that day on Dafydd shame
    Unless he make his song!

GREEN MASS

And wasn't it a pleasant place today
Listening under a cloak of fine green leaves
To the skilled thrush singing out his polished lay
How pretty those bright notes, what pattern's weave!
Sent from Carmarthen sweet, this messenger,
At the behest of love, my golden haired,
From her a most delightful harbinger,
Her love in Nanterch dingle to be shared.
Under the trees, the tender flowers of May,
The green wings of the wind make God's altar;
Morfudd sent this brown gospeller to pray,
His holy wafer a green leaf, psalter
A branching tree, Mass bell, a bird song gay;
Our praise rose high to Him, Creator!

DOPPELGÄNGER

Yesterday I sheltered beneath clean leaves
Of sweetest green, a cloak of kindest birch;
The sky was throwing water down in sheaves
And I by Gwen left waiting in the lurch.

Of all a sudden standing face to face
A figure stood beside my side; trembling
I crossed myself, my heart with quickened pace;
'What are you, ghost-man-resembling?'

'I am your dark shadow, for Mary sake'
Be silent till I tell you why I'm here;
I want to tell you the figure you make
In others' eyes, the sight that you appear.'

'Why should you, foul and shrinking creature, seek
To follow me around, who pays your hire?
You long-legged scarecrow why do you peek
At everything I do, you drowned-in-mire?'

'I am no foul ghost, no chimera
But come to see you and to mark your deeds,
Fear not me, I am your familiar
Who knows your wants and all your fickle needs!'

'Then what, you foul and doddering spirit old,
Is your purpose, you lumping shape of scrag,
You bloated bogey, like a monk in mould,
You heap of darkness like a blackened hag!'

'Feeble and weak though I may seem to you,
I keep an eye on your deceitful tricks;
No movement of your day is straight or true
To me, we are as close as sheep and ticks.'

'How dare you spy on my you filthy wreck
What faults I have are known to all the world;
I've not sold my country, nor done a stretch
Or been caught with another's woman curled!'

'But if I said a tithe I knew, your life
Would not be worth a light!'
      'Away be got!
I'll have you on the point of my black knife,
Constrict your tongue within a hangman's knot!'

THE BOG

Miserable poet, fear-filled, harassed
And stumbling in the darkest bog of night;
How come out alive, what fiends amassed
To seize me with their treachery and might!
Oh tardy-rising moon, why is the sun
Hidden from the poet and all his fame;
Should my enemies find me here how run,
How scape with life, my horse and my good name?
What's worse, if drowned where would my reverence
Find home? Sunk with me in the foulest peat
With Gwyn-the-Mist, and no deliverance.
In getting out my horse misplaced his feet
And ruined my Caernarvon stockings bright —
Though now I'm free, O Bog, I bless you quite!

THE LOAN

I trysted in the May brushwood
(Lissom Dafydd, handsome girl)
An honest maiden fair and good
Kisses I gave were not from churl
Kisses she sought eagerly
Returning six for every three.

But bolder far than I this maid
And challenged me in lovers' sport
With such vigour that I prayed
For time in case that I got caught
She taking arrows from my bow
Before I had the time to know.

But from her there was no escape
My fate was sealed without a fight!
'Rude Dafydd, by your manly shape
You'll surely win your prize tonight;
You came again for that embrace
Wherein both parties win the race!'

'You know I come for pleasure's sake
I do not want to wrest the prize
Or from you force a maiden's break
Nor make a woman in men's eyes —
Foolish creature you must know
I wouldn't use a maiden so!'

'No one shall say I did unmaid
(Even for Mary's sake I won't!)
Furthermore I am afraid
To give your father an affront
Having already just survived
His harsh tongue on my gentle hide.'

'Stop your dissembling you rogue
Nature shows us what to do
And in the Spring it is in vogue
The meadow sweet will suit us two
Or byre or barn is safe enough
Who cares the mattress might be rough?'

'This easy-going pleasure's fine
But brings relations' blackened wrath
And though archdeacon's goodness shines
Excommunication's path
Could well be mine unless I paid
Forty shillings for this trade.'

'Mean and nasty Dafydd you are
Here on the bank under the trees;
A good Welshman go so far
Have a maid on bended knees
And for the lack of forty shilling
Refuse a girl who's more than willing?'

'What if I have not shillings free
Upon this pleasant summer's day?'
'Sure I'll lend them most promptly
And I'll give you time to pay!'
All my excuses were in vain
The maiden lost the women's gain.

THE MIRROR

I looked into the mirror and was shocked –
Monstrous discovery! I was not fair;
But the mirror spoke plain and I was mocked.
For sake of Enid's brow, my cheeks show wear
From lamentation and are pinched, and thin,
And you could make a razor from my nose.
Even the brightness of my eye is dim
And handfuls of my hair fall to my toes.
Perhaps I am bewitched, or could I be
Some dragon-fiend – or could the mirror lie?
If mirror's true and this is really me
Better than this creature were to die.
The mirror like the moon shines prettily
A cruel witch's trick to fool the eye.

THE HARD ROAD

Did ever a man in his wooing
      Walk as I have done with leaden pace
Desolated and forsaken
      For one fair face?

At our last meeting only sorrow
      And more pain at the tryst at Meirch
When seeking her gold loveliness,
      I crossing Eleirch.

Bitterly sighed I in Bleddyn bower
      Where she coldly refused me
By Maesaleg's running water
      I spoke my love boldly.

For her sake crossed I have Bergul
      Its treacherous boiling water
And blessed Meibion Dafydd passed
      For this mother's daughter.

Gladly I've gone to her in love
      Though much in pain from loving her
And for a sight of gold-spun hair
      Been snapped at by cur.

Across to Camallt and to Rhiw
      And viewed from there spreading valley
And passed swiftly through Cyflaen
      With her to dally.

But nowhere do I see her move
    Stealthily at my yearning side
When eagerly in summertime
    I trailed my pride.

I pushed through Cwcwll hollow
    Skirting the ring of Gastell Gwrgan
And crossed the gosling-feeding reeds
    Where time began.

Below the walls of Adail Heilyn
    I limped like an exhausted hound
And lurked about Ifor's Court
    And nothing found.

Hid like a monk within the choir
    I sought my sweet Morfudd to meet
With no hope of a sight of her
    My nimble sweet.

On every side of Nant-y-glo
    I've sought where my love might be hid
In company with Gwynn-the-Mist,
    No witty Ovid.

In Gwern-y-Talwyrn only did
    My hand bring my love to my side
And where we lay there was a cloak
    Of leaves to hide.

In that bleak place no green grass grew
    Nor shrub or plant of any kind
On trodden leaves on Adam's track
    Was true love twined.

Bitter is a troubled man's soul
    Lacking the embrace of his love
Bitter the road his body treads
    No heaven above!

THE MOUSE

More fickle than a straw the girl I love
You cannot credit anything she says
More than the word of Mouse from beam above
That fell into the vat of beer. To praise
The cat, it leapt quickly into the beer
And raised the mouse's head lest it should choke,
The mouse swearing an oath out of its fear
Which he renounced when safe, and made a joke.
'You must keep your word,' demanded the cat
When Mouse was safely hidden in the thatch;
'Not so,' he said, 'when I was in the vat,
Drunk as an owl, I trusted you to catch
Me from the flood'; so, tit-for-tat
Gwen and a drunken mouse are a good match.

THE WINDOW

Like as to music was my love
And my embrace a wanton song
Under broad branches, leaves above
My beauty slept and knew no wrong
        Framed by the oaks, my little dove!

But when I sought another kiss
Through her narrow oaken window
She spurned my offer and my bliss
Was dashed as if a sudden blow
        Came at me with a warning hiss!

And that old window which lets through
The sun and moon obstructed me
Ugly old window how can I woo
Through your narrow timbered tree
        True love seeks a wide window true!

Your narrow frame set up a fire
Within, such as that passion which
Took Melwas when his burning ire
Reached such an intolerant pitch
        His very heart became a pyre!

And as he came from Caerleon
Fearing nothing in his way
Cogyfran Gawr's daughter won
And nothing would his will gainsay
        A path I'm timid to take on!

Without the hope of jewel face
Without the light of any star
My heart's anger has quickened pace
The window frame becomes a bar
    And prison to my sublime grace.

Our noses cannot gently brush
Nor can our lips come kiss-to-sip
But only up against wood crush
With Melwas' strength I'd lattice rip
    And eagerly the window rush.

No one has been so tormented
Sat sleepless by an oak window
From his love been so prevented
Devil take it and break it so
    Its frame and joists are wrested!

Anger and salt tears took me outside
And killed my song, until my hand
Took up a saw which stealth applied
Vigorously, till nothing banned
    My entrance and my loved one's side!

MANAFON DINGLE

Dyddgu shining brilliant creature
      With soft dark falling hair
Your secret lover would meet you
      In Manafon Dingle fair

Here will be no coarse rough food
      No gluttonous eating
No porridge, stirabout, tough meat
      Nor incautious feasting

Nor have I invited Englishmen
      With loud and drunken friends
Nor labourers just come of age
      Marking puberty's end

No, I promise you but mead
      The song of nightingale
The brown-backed nightingale, and thrush
      Bird songs to regale

The nightingale, melodious thrush
      To sing with dual tongue
A chorus for our ears alone
      Their night and daytime song

We shall lie under the leaves
      The splendid trees above
While the birds sport in high branches
      And celebrate our love

Ringed about us are nine trees
    The finest in the wood
They make a bower for our bed
    Our quilt the clover good

Here can we lie without trouble
    Where gentle roebucks feed
You and I at peace together
    Sipping our lovers' mead

Where birds sing I am glad, where builds
    The blackbird his strong nest
Where stands the tall majestic trees
    Where better than to rest?

Where better than this dwelling-place
    The paradise of leaves
To bless our sweet and ready passion
    Beneath kind Nature's eaves!

Pale light in shade of hanging branches
    Still water, smokeless air
No scraggy beggars disturb peace
    There shall we both repair

Myself only and my bright girl
    She of the glow-worm eyes
White skin of the falling wave
    We'll sup tonight love's prize.

WELSH STUDIES

1. Michael Price, **The Account Book for the Borough of Swansea, Wales, 1640-1660: A Study in Local Administration During the Civil War and Interregnum**
2. Peter Morris, **The Days of Visitation: A Practical and Statistical Study of the Parishes of the Diocese of Swansea and Brecon Based on the Returns to the Visitation Questionnaires of Bishop Vaughan From 1977-1987**
3. D. Ben Rees, **The Life and Work of Owen Thomas, 1812-1891: A Welsh Preacher in Liverpool**
4. Gavin Edwards and Graham Sumner (eds.), **The Historical and Cultural Connections and Parallels Between Wales and Australia**
5. Brynley F. Roberts, **Studies on Middle Welsh Literature**
6. J. Gwynfor Jones (golygydd), **Agweddau ar Dwf Piwritaniaeth yng Nghymru yn yr Ail Ganrif ar Bymtheg.**
7. Rachel Bromwich and D. Simon Evans (Compiled by), **Glossary to** *Culhwch ac Olwen.*
8. Francis R. Phillips, **Creating an Education System for England and Wales**
9. Martin Green, **Homage to Dafydd ap Gwilym**